The author wishes to thank the photographers and photo agencies who contributed the photographs (all under copyright) to this book:

Magnum Photos/Abbas p. 10 left, Richard Klavar p. 1, Eric Lessing p. 14, Wayne Miller p. 9, Marilyn Silverstone p. 21, Dennis Stock p. 17; Nancy Sheehan p. 26; SuperStock, Inc./Scott Barrow p. 29, Kurt Scholz p. 23, Ned Valentin p. 27 top; Valan Photos/John Eastcott & Yva Momatiuk p. 7, Val & Alan Wilkinson p. 13; Viesti Associates/Michael Lewis p. 8 right, 11, Craig Lovell p. 16, Eleni Mylonas p. 5, 22, Joe Viesti back cover, Edward G. Young p. 28; Woodfin Camp & Associates/Alexandria Avakian p. 25, Bernard Boutrit front cover, David Burnett p. 4, John Eastcott & Yva Momatiuk p. 6, 10 right, 24, 27 bottom, Chuck Fishman p. 2, Kal Muller p. 15, A. Reiniger p. 8 left, Israel Talby p. 12, 18, 19, 20.

Printed in Hong Kong by South China Printing Company (1988) Ltd.
4 5 6 7 8 9 10
Library of Congress Cataloging in Publication Data
Morris, Ann. Weddings / by Ann Morris.
   p.   cm. Summary: A picture book provides a simple introduction to the things that often happen at a wedding.
ISBN 0-688-13272-3. — ISBN 0-688-13273-1 (lib. bdg.) 1. Marriage customs and rites—Juvenile literature.
[1. Marriage customs and rites. 2. Weddings.] I. Title.
GT2665.M65 1995 391.5—dc20 94-48040 CIP AC(CIP)

ANN MORRIS

WEDDINGS

LOTHROP, LEE & SHEPARD BOOKS

NEW YORK

4

All over the world, a wedding is a very special celebration.

It is the time when a man and a woman promise to spend the rest of their lives together.

Weddings can be plain or fancy . . .

indoors or outdoors . . .

but they are always special occasions.

Family and friends want to be there.

Everyone dresses up —

15

especially the bride and groom.

Here come the bride and groom —on foot,

in a car,

or a boat,

even on an elephant!

The bride and groom promise to love and care
for each other always.

They may say a prayer together

or share a special food.

Sometimes they exchange rings or a kiss.

After the ceremony, there is food and music and dancing.

Often there are gifts for the bride and groom. Always there are everyone's wishes for a long and happy life together.

INDEX

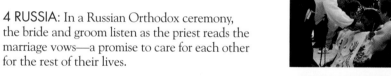

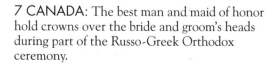

15 INDONESIA: Attendants cool the bride and groom with fans during a wedding on tropical Sumbawa Island.

23 THAILAND: A Bangkok couple are linked by a strand of yarn during their wedding to symbolize how love binds them together.

16 INDIA: This Kashmiri bride and groom wear necklaces of money to show that they can afford to be married and take on the responsibilities of family life.

24 SLOVAKIA: The traditional wedding meal for a Slovak bride and groom is sausages, which are supposed to bring them many children.

17 GHANA: Many Moslems believe it is proper to cover the head in public. The modest bride is veiled from head to toe.

25 RUSSIA: This Jewish couple wear rings to remind them of their marriage vows. A wedding ring is usually worn on the third finger of the left hand.

18 SOUTH AFRICA: A bright flock of bridesmaids and a flower girl escort a wedding couple to church.

26 UNITED STATES: A bride dances with her flower girls.

19 JAPAN: This bride is wearing a style of dress that is centuries old to be married in a Shinto rite at Heian Shrine in Kyoto.

27 IRAN: Everyone dances at a wedding!

20 SWEDEN: A church boat ferries the bride across Lake Siljan to her wedding.

27 SLOVAKIA: Passersby stop to watch as Gypsy musicians lead a wedding procession through the streets.

21 INDIA: A bride is carried in a palanquin through the streets of Jaipur. The groom follows, riding an elephant.

28 UNITED STATES: Family and friends bring gifts to help this Navaho bride and groom furnish their first home.

22 INDIA: The dot of red powder on this Hindu bride's forehead is called a *kumkum*.

29 UNITED STATES: Throwing rice at the newlyweds is a way to wish them a long, happy life together and many children.

Where in the world were these photographs taken?

For Ethan and Dana, as we pray together – J.B.

For Mali – L.F.

Acknowledgements

page 6: Traditional. Page 7: Anonymous. Page 8: Edith Rutter Leatham (1870-1939). Page 9: Traditional. Pages 10-11: 1st verse traditional, 2nd verse © Jeremy Brooks. Page 12: 18th-century German hymn translated into English as 'We Plough the Fields and Scatter'. Page 13: Traditional Cherokee blessing. Page 14: From *The Prayer Garden: An Anthology of Children's Prayers*, Christopher Herbert, Bishop of St Albans. Page 15: 'A Child's Prayer' from *Children's Prayers from Around the World*, ed. Mary Batchelor (Lion, 1977). Page 16: Traditional. Page 17: Paramahansa Yogananda, founder of Self-Realisation Fellowship (1893-1952). Pages 18-19: Victor Hugo (1802-85). Page 20: © The United Educators, Inc. Page 21: English translation, from the opera *Hänsel und Gretel*, Engelbert Humperdinck (1854-1921). The publishers apologise to any copyright holders they were unable to trace and would like to hear from them.

My First Prayers copyright © Frances Lincoln Limited 2008
Text copyright © Jeremy Brooks 2008
Illustrations copyright © Laure Fournier 2008

First published in Great Britain in 2008 and the USA in 2009 by
Frances Lincoln Children's Books, 4 Torriano Mews,
Torriano Avenue, London NW5 2RZ
www.franceslincoln.com

British Library Cataloguing in Publication Data
available on request

ISBN: 978-1-84507-535-4

Illustrated with watercolours, acrylics and pencil

Set in Stone Informal

Printed in Singapore
9 8 7 6 5 4 3 2 1

My First Prayers

Selected by *The Reverend Jeremy Brooks*

Illustrated by Laure Fournier

FRANCES LINCOLN
CHILDREN'S BOOKS

O God, my Father, stay always with me.
In the morning, in the evening,
by day or by night, always be my helper.

Poland

Keep my little tongue today,
keep it gentle while I play.
Keep my hands from doing wrong,
keep my feet the whole day long.
Keep me all, O Jesus mild,
keep me ever thy dear child.

USA

Thank you for the world so sweet,
thank you for the food we eat,
thank you for the birds that sing –
thank you, God, for everything.

England

God is great, God is good,
let us thank him for our food.

USA

Dear Jesus, bless my hands today,
and may the things they do
be kind and loving, strong and good,
two busy hands for you.

Dear Jesus, bless my every deed
and guide each word I say.
Help me, Lord, to work for you
and do my best today.

England

All good gifts around us
are sent from heaven above.
Then thank the Lord,
O thank the Lord
for all his love.

Germany

May the warm winds of heaven
blow softly upon your house.
May the Great Spirit
bless all who enter there.
May your moccasins
make happy tracks in many snows,
and may the rainbow
always touch your shoulder.

Native America

For buckets and spades, for sunshine and shade,
for sand in the toes, for cream on the nose,
for jumping the tide, for having a ride,
for laughter and fun, praise God, everyone.

England

Thank God for rain
and the beautiful rainbow colours,
and thank God for letting children
splash in the puddles.

England

O God, look on us and be always with us,
that we may live happily.

South Africa

Naughty or good, I am your child.

India

Good night! Good night!
Far flies the light,
but still God's love
shall flame above,
making all bright.
Good night! Good night!

France

Sleep my little one!
The night is all wind and rain;
The meal has been wet
by the raindrops
and bent is the sugar cane;
O Giver who gives to the people,
in safety my little son keep!
My little son with the head-dress,
sleep, sleep, sleep!

East Africa

When at night I go to sleep
fourteen angels watch do keep.
Two my head are guarding,
two my feet are guiding,
two are on my right hand,
two are on my left hand,
two who warmly cover,
two who o'er me hover,
two to whom is given
to guide my steps to Heaven.

Germany